violence, poverty, provincialism) conspire to subvert the human quest for wholeness, harmony, and beauty.

But Mississippi is also, as a number of these poems remind us, the land of Faulkner, the land where imagination and poetic genius can transcend and thus triumph over sordid fact. The parallel is undoubtedly intentional. Like Faulkner, Brodsky's protagonist lovingly wrestles with polysyllabic words and a sometimes tortuous syntax to fashion a poetry to live by. And herein lies the uniqueness of Brodsky's handling of the Quest motif. For his protagonist, who rightly suspects that . . . uprootedness itself is my destiny, / I its tribal apprentice, plying deserts forever . . . the end of the journey is not a place but a state of heightened awareness that can only be expressed as poetry — a poetry that (like Brodsky's style) teaches one

> . . . *how to hold Time's quicksilver sands,*
> *Control those wildly ephemeral moments*
> *When poetry and prose would rapidly fuse,*
> *Then slowly come undone*
> *In the most wondrous sundering of flesh and*
>   *emotion . . .*

This part of Brodsky's message, of course, is far from negative. For poetry, as we all know, is not only the beginning of wisdom; it can also be the first halting step toward salvation.

— Robert Hamblin, author of *From the Ground Up: Poems of One Southerner's Passage to Adulthood*

American obsession with Traveling, with Moving On, with Leaving Here and Going There.

Louis Daniel Brodsky's *Disappearing in Mississippi Latitudes* both repeats and revises this central American myth of journey and discovery. From the opening words, "Fleeing Farmington," to the last line, when his protagonist, weeping, is "Home again to my empty temple," Brodsky fuses the American experience with that of the Wandering Jew in a treatment that raises crucial questions of responsibility and freedom, engagement or flight. The middle volume of a trilogy tracing an outlander's love-hate relationship with Mississippi, *Disappearing* chronicles the point at which the somewhat romanticized and naive view of place and self expressed in Volume I, *Mississippi Vistas*, gives way to a more somber and honest assessment. The result, presented in a series of interior monologues that combine the emotional power of poetry with suspenseful design of fiction, is poignant and painful yet also, occasionally, as in "Intimations of Immortality in Spring" and "Haunting Voices," encouraging and hopeful.

However, while it has its positive moments, this is not a happy book. It is a book which applies the child's fear of getting lost to the terrors of adulthood; it is a book about disappearing, not about finding oneself or being found. In these gripping and troubling poems Mississippi is characterized as a place that deflates the spirit and kills the dream. Here both nature (punishing heat and humidity, river floods, thunderstorms, suffocating kudzu) and man (racial prejudice, bigotry, violence, poverty, provincialism) conspire to subvert the human quest for wholeness, harmony, and beauty.

But Mississippi is also, as a number of these poems remind us, the land of Faulkner, the land where imagination and poetic genius can transcend and thus triumph over sordid fact. The parallel is undoubtedly intentional. Like Faulkner, Brodsky's protagonist lovingly wrestles with polysyllabic words and a sometimes-tortuous syntax to fashion a poetry to live by. And herein lies the uniqueness of Brodsky's handling of the Quest motif. For his protagonist, who rightly suspects that " . . . uprootedness itself is my destiny, / I its tribal apprentice, plying deserts forever," the end of the journey is not a place but a state of heightened awareness that can only be expressed as poetry — a poetry that (like Brodsky's style) teaches one

> . . . *how to hold Time's quicksilver sands,*
> *Control those wildly ephemeral moments*
> *When poetry and prose would rapidly fuse,*
> *Then slowly come undone*
> *In the most wondrous sundering of flesh and emotion: . . .*

This part of Brodsky's message, of course, is far from negative. For poetry, as we all know, is not only the beginning of wisdom; it can also be the first halting step toward salvation.
— Robert Hamblin, author of *From the Ground Up: Poems of One Southerner's Passage to Adulthood*

L.D. Brodsky's poetic trilogy is saturated with his empathy for William Faulkner and his Oxford, Mississippi, but the brilliant resonance of the poems comes from the poet's recognition that Mississippi was not only Faulkner terrain but also what he calls "Ku Klux Kudzu." From this witch's brew, Brodsky has crafted both a hymn to the novelist and a cautionary tale with profound social and personal implications. He has succeeded in carving out his own Yoknapatawpha.
— Frederick R. Karl, author of *William Faulkner: American Writer* and *Joseph Conrad: The Three Lives*

Disappearing in Mississippi Latitudes establishes Louis Daniel Brodsky firmly in the front rank of contemporary American poets. This is not a "collection" of poems; it is a brilliantly crafted story told in poetic form, a story about a gifted artist's journey through the world of Faulkner country that will leave you gasping in awe. Brodsky's overriding honesty, his command of language and metaphor, his lyrical insights into the landscape of Mississippi both past and present, make his verse a national treasure. I hope that every literate American will read this powerful book.
— Stephen B. Oates, Robert F. Kennedy Memorial Book and Christopher awards winner and author of *William Faulkner: The Man and the Artist* and *Let the Trumpet Sound: A Life of Martin Luther King, Jr.*

Brodsky's verse is steeped in the sensuous brew of the North Mississippi country, and the mixture of ingredients — what he finds there, what it tells him about himself — makes for memorable poems.
— Louis D. Rubin, Jr., Editor of *The Literary South*

With the publication of *Disappearing in Mississippi Latitudes*, the second volume of his remarkable *Mississippi Trilogy*, Louis Daniel Brodsky completes the story of the fatal attraction of the Mississippi of the last great modern romantic, William Faulkner, for the Jewish poet of tempestuously romantic temperament he has created to tell the story in the trilogy . . . *Disappearing in Mississippi Latitudes* fills in the chronicle of the poet's decline by detailing some of the moods and moments in the drama of the poet's transit from romantic enthusiasm, introduced in *Mississippi Vistas*, to the degraded state of consciousness he depicts in *Mistress Mississippi*, . . . In a way, *A Mississippi Trilogy* is about the ironic situation of a poet who is overwhelmed by his admiration for, and his jealously of, a literary genius he cannot hope to emulate. In a deeper sense it is a story about the alienation of the poet in modern history: it is about the Faulkner who, in his alienation, found his most memorable character in the poet Quentin Compson, who lived his brief life in the tension between hating what he loved and loving what he hated. But, more profoundly, *A Mississippi Trilogy* is about the alienation of the "profligate Jew" who tells the story, a poet whose tortured sensibility is informed by his inescapable awareness of a centuries old inheritance of displacement and alienation, and who ironically possesses a knowledge as intense as Faulkner's of what is at once the destructive yet strangely sustaining power of hating what one loves and loving what one hates. Brodsky's trilogy is an achievement to be reckoned with.

> — Lewis P. Simpson, author of *The Dispossessed Garden: Pastoral and History in Southern Literature*

Louis Daniel Brodsky has created a deeply felt personal response to both William Faulkner and the Mississippi Delta. The poems are imbued with a sense of time and place. His great admiration for Faulkner and his love of the deep south shines through each poem. In addition many poems capture the intensity of the Civil Rights movement of the 50s and 60s and reveal great sensitivity to the urgent issues of race that remain with us today.

> — Meta D. Wilde, coauthor of *A Loving Gentleman: The Story of William Faulkner and Meta Carpenter*

What happens when deep sensitivity and high intelligence meet on the middle ground of daily life and find no place to rest? L.D. Brodsky moves and stops and moves again like a bead of mercury on the ever-tilting surface of the lower Mississippi basin. This begins his poetry.

> — Joel Williamson, Robert F. Kennedy Memorial Book and Parkman awards winner and author of *William Faulkner & Southern History* and *The Crucible of Race: Black-White Relations in the American South Since Emancipation*

DISAPPEARING IN MISSISSIPPI LATITUDES

VOLUME TWO of
A MISSISSIPPI TRILOGY

Books by
LOUIS DANIEL BRODSKY

Poetry
Trilogy: A Birth Cycle   (1974)
Monday's Child   (1975)
The Kingdom of Gewgaw   (1976)
Point of Americas II   (1976)
Preparing for Incarnations   (1976)
La Preciosa   (1977)
Stranded in the Land of Transients   (1978)
The Uncelebrated Ceremony of Pants Factory Fatso   (1978)
Birds in Passage   (1980)
Résumé of a Scrapegoat   (1980)
Mississippi Vistas: Volume One of *A Mississippi Trilogy*   (1983) (1990)
You Can't Go Back, Exactly   (1988)
The Thorough Earth   (1989)
Four and Twenty Blackbirds Soaring   (1989)
Falling from Heaven: Holocaust Poems of a Jew and a Gentile
   (with William Heyen)   (1991)
Forever, for Now: Poems for a Later Love   (1991)
Mistress Mississippi: Volume Three of *A Mississippi Trilogy*   (1992)
A Gleam in the Eye: Poems for a First Baby   (1992)
Gestapo Crows: Holocaust Poems   (1992)
The Capital Café: Poems of Redneck, U.S.A.   (1993)
Disappearing in Mississippi Latitudes:
   Volume Two of *A Mississippi Trilogy*   (1994)

Bibliography (Coedited with Robert Hamblin)
Selections from the William Faulkner Collection of Louis Daniel Brodsky:
   A Descriptive Catalogue   (1979)
Faulkner: A Comprehensive Guide to the Brodsky Collection
      Volume I: The Biobibliography   (1982)
      Volume II: The Letters   (1984)
      Volume III: The De Gaulle Story   (1984)
      Volume IV: Battle Cry   (1985)
      Volume V: Manuscripts and Documents   (1989)
Country Lawyer and Other Stories for the Screen by William
   Faulkner   (1987)
Stallion Road: A Screenplay by William Faulkner   (1989)

Biography
William Faulkner, Life Glimpses   (1990)

DISAPPEARING IN MISSISSIPPI LATITUDES

VOLUME TWO of
A MISSISSIPPI TRILOGY

Poems by

Louis Daniel Brodsky

Louis Daniel Brodsky
12/28/07
St. Louis, M

TIME BEING BOOKS®
POETRY IN SIGHT AND SOUND

Time Being Books®
10411 Clayton Road
St. Louis, Missouri 63131

Time Being Books® volumes are printed on acid-free paper, and binding
materials are chosen for strength and durability.

Time Being Books® is an imprint of Time Being Press, Inc.
St. Louis, Missouri

Library of Congress Cataloging-in-Publication Data:

Brodsky, Louis Daniel.
    Disappearing in Mississippi latitudes : poems / by Louis Daniel
Brodsky. — 1st ed.
      p. cm. — (A Mississippi trilogy ; v. 2)
    ISBN 1-877770-80-9 (alk. paper) : ISBN 1-877770-81-7
(pbk. : alk. paper) : ISBN 1-877770-82-5 (audio cassette)
      1. Mississippi — Poetry. I. Title. II. Series: Brodsky, Louis Daniel.
Mississippi trilogy ; v. 2.
PS3552.R623M5   1994
811'.54 — dc20   94-28822

                                                            CIP

Book design and typesetting by Lori Loesche
Manufactured in the United States of America

First Edition, first printing (December 1994)

I wish to make grateful acknowledgment to these publications, in which the following poems, in earlier versions, originally appeared: *The Cape Rock* ("Inundation," "Street Cleaner"); *Publications of the Missouri Philological Association* ("Blown Off Course"); *Images* ("Implacable Impasse," "Jogging Bailey's Woods"); and *Anthology of Magazine Verse and Yearbook of American Poetry*, 1985 edition ("Inundation").

The epigraph for this book is from *Absalom, Absalom!* by William Faulkner. Copyright © 1936 by William Faulkner. Copyright renewed 1964 by Estelle Faulkner and Jill Faulkner Summers. Reprinted by permission of Random House, Inc.

I am appreciative of Jerry Call, Sheri Vandermolen, and Lori Loesche, members of the editorial staff of Time Being Books, and Professor Robert Hamblin of Southeast Missouri State University, for having enhanced my manuscript with their incisive suggestions as I prepared this book for publication.

For

Cleanth Brooks
Malcolm Cowley
Lewis P. Simpson
and
Robert Penn Warren

"Now I want you to tell me just one thing more. Why do you hate the South?"

"I dont hate it," Quentin said, quickly, at once, immediately; "I dont hate it," he said. *I dont hate it* he thought, panting in the cold air, the iron New England dark; *I dont. I dont! I dont hate it! I dont hate it!*

— from *Absalom, Absalom!*, William Faulkner

Contents

DISAPPEARING IN MISSISSIPPI LATITUDES

VOLUME TWO of

A MISSISSIPPI TRILOGY

Chapter One

BOUND SOUTH OUT OF TIME

* This symbol is used to indicate that a stanza has been divided because of pagination.

Making Another Desert Trek

Fleeing Farmington this Friday morning,
I cut across country,
Chasing undulant Highway 32.
My urgency engenders nervousness,
Worry, guilt on leaving home again
After myriad recent excursions to St. Louis
In search of a house to rent.
Rain plots against vision,
Whose peregrine soul
Defies tradition, discipline, ethics,
Premeditated destinations, and goals.

My eyes keep to the road, I to myself,
Inaccessible except to an incidental few,
Who see only my disguises.
Whenever I return from remote regions,
Feeling as relieved as a freed prisoner of war,
My wife's shortness, derision, scorn
Immediately reincarcerate my heart.
Even my children fail to recognize Daddy
Clad in tatterdemalion poet-clothes,
Satchel brimming with Diaspora-verses
In the keys of Whitman and de Tocqueville.

Gifts, kisses, trite insights
Don't hold sway anymore,
Yet love, or its essence, lingers.
Yes! Yes! We both know it,
Although its once-vibrant core-flames
Sputter in caves we've dredged
With lips, tongues, claws this lost, last decade,
Fighting to retain Youth's innocence,
Easy-reasoned omniscience, and sensual elegance
We nourished reading to each other
This Is My Beloved and *The Prophet*.

What is it, then, I question
On these incessant trips out from the center,
Bereft of my blessed children
*

And dazed helpmate,
That keeps repelling us, forcing me to flee
My former sources of peaceful repose,
Family and sanctuarial home?
After all this desolate time away,
I yet have no guess
Unless uprootedness itself is my destiny,
I its tribal apprentice, plying deserts forever.

White Backlash

Lands that less than three weeks ago
Were crowded with cotton stalks
Dripping liquid fluff
Now either are disced into furrowed oblivion
Or, having been picked clean,
Resemble potter's fields
Littered with brittle crucifixes
Shivering in the heated breeze.

Only soybean crops
Strut and flaunt their stuff like peacocks
In this end-of-September season
Below Hayti, Caruthersville,
On down toward Braggadocio and Memphis.
Even these, usually green as watercress in a stream,
Seem to have been drenched in urine
By a mythic Swiftian colossus.

As my tired eyes drift southerly,
My spirit begins to unwind,
Leaving behind memories for my wife and two children
To protect against my parasitical guilt.
Systematically, it jettisons reason and intellect
To help counter resistance to the new seed
I've come to broadcast: Abolition —
A hybrid variety from Boston, Detroit, St. Louis.

Dozing Off

Driving south this shimmering September morn,
My head droops
Like a man-high black-eyed Susan.

Solitude is the hitchhiker
I picked up miles back,
Praying conversation might keep me awake,

But my eyes still refuse to make contact
With his uncommunicative face
As the highway lullabies us strangers

Into the concrete mantra of whining tires.
Gradually I submit to drowsiness,
Sink deeply and deeper

Into the incantatory ululation
The road wails to wayward navigators
While luring their souls away from home.

Suddenly time and distance
Relinquish their holds, loose me;
I come uncocooned, exit this dead mood

That has imprisoned me for 200 miles,
Confiscated from memory the preceding four hours.
I breathe in, suspire;

A fresh view snaps my neck erect.
Ahead, I detect the river
Connecting Arkansas with Tennessee.

Instinctively, I speed up,
Relieved to be arriving intact, back again
Where ghosts masquerade as sunflowers.

Rehearsing in Purgatory

Having evacuated my bittersweet, insular purlieu
260 miles back
And exchanged it for this seething heat
Infused with vague hypochondriacal fears
Stabbing at my ulcerous gut
Like a goose pecking buttons off the sleeve
Of an arm extended to feed it,
I course down I-55, below Memphis, toward Oxford.
Not knowing why I've come
Or whose necromantic prophecy I'll fulfill,
I put in my silent appearance
As though I were the South's menstrual seed
Traveling down its interstate tubes
Toward conception, creation,
Doomed to abort
Or, at best, miscarry any poetry
That might accidentally attach
To the lining of my imagination's uterus.

Swamps congested with cypress and gum stumps
Enter consciousness through my eyes;
Vision is inundated with moccasin-phobias
Slithering through its fluted convolutions.
Although I choose to regard threats of lynching,
Swastikas, and Joe Christmas castrations
As phantasms extinct as saurians,
My heart can't quit spasming.
Something about this mid-South
Transfigures my romantic illusions
Into chimeras who stalk me
Even as I infiltrate their domain
Waving a white flag.
Something would have me witness firsthand
My own craven ruination
For accepting exile to the spirit's Elba
As a trial by which I might decide
Whether my sanity can withstand an eternity
*

Creating verse for recitation by the unredeemed.
Something would have me embrace confinement to Hades
Despite being able to write paeans to angels,
Panegyrics and odes to saints,
Benedictions to myself as God's earthly surrogate.

Ritual Disappearance

Dislocated between daybreak and noon,
I, the scribe for the Tribe of Abraham,
Wander distractedly south,
Still in range of FM 100,
Listening to Memphis' enchanting voice:
Steely Dan's "Deacon Blues"
And Randy Newman's "Rednecks"
Jew-diciously slotted between prolix advertisements
For Mud Island and the Peabody Hotel.

I drown in innocuous sounds;
My minimal images smolder at ignition point
Like fired piles of wet leaves.
I'm not used to so much freedom,
Accruing from this Friday
I've embezzled from my rigid work ethic.
Rarely have I shirked duties,
Left town without notifying someone
Where emergency could reach me.

I can't fathom the preternatural fiat
That's commanded me to abandon moorings,
Pull from under my psyche
The spare rug I always keep under the rug
I'm forever pulling from beneath my feet.
Yet in this oblique, philistine wilderness,
Mississippi,
I fear distant voices
Shrinking into their sheets as I near Oxford.

Not habitually given to superstition,
Visions, or divinations from self-ordained mystics,
I grope this day for any clue
To what might have caused me to flee,
A mere unacknowledged poet
Who augments his paltry income
Teaching part-time at a junior college.
Suddenly, I recall why Choctaws and Chickasaws
Used to go off to the woods to die.

Killer Sun

As I press toward my final destination,
The killer sun,
Skimming noon's shallows in search of prey,
Spies my movements, swims my way,
Bites me to squinting;
My eyes bleed crow's-feet, go blurry,
As if death and darkness have abruptly converged;
Fingers and toes freeze.
Loblolly pines lining both sides of I-55
Cast a gray-blue shadow
Through which I drive in plain sight
Of the insanely circling sun,
Wondering why I've been singled out,
Condemned to surrender to an enemy
I've never provoked, let alone seen up close.

I ignore Hurricane Creek's dirty surface,
Disappear below the Tallahatchie's grim shimmer.
Soon, the Batesville turnoff looms.
I exit, head east toward Oxford,
A maimed spirit hoping to reach shore
Before nothing of me remains
In Mississippi
Except the promise to my wife,
That I'd be very careful driving,
Resonating in my memories of her
And the vaguely courageous concession I made
On leaving home much earlier this a.m.
To be wary of staring down adversaries,
Even if I might wipe them from sight
Just by shading my eyes with my hand.

Performing Inordinate Rituals

This 90-degree September day,
I dash over Oxford's streets
In jogging shoes and shorts.
A carefree, bare-chested tightrope walker
Showing off his death-defying capriciousness,
I cast aside disbelief,
Spring through blazing hoops like a trained lion
Instinctively placing its feet in sequence.

Despite fatigue and the ephemeral realities
Looming in afternoon's wings like a Greek chorus
Humming late summer's doomed, lugubrious plaints,
I run, jump from sidewalk to alley,
Lope through ravines of Bailey's Woods
Even the most exuberant butterfly
Might not choose to navigate
Nor modern-day Nijinsky leap.

Neither mystical nor physical forces
Traduce my fragile muse
This suspiciously too-warm season
Or reduce my spirit to prostituting its fancy dance
Merely by engendering skepticism,
Making intuition accuse sleazy Lorelei
Of being back on the streets again
To solicit favors from unsuspecting bums like me.

Nothing, it seems, can distract me
From spinning my spirit's spectacular pirouettes,
Forgetting just exactly who I'm supposed to be,
For what reason I drove to Oxford today,
And when I actually metamorphosed.
Only my bones know for certain
Why this urgent celebration has occurred:
The days of butterflies and lions are circumscribed.

Isolated at the Oasis

The shape of my spirit and the space it occupies
Are recognized by few here in Oxford;
They are amazed by its shameless nakedness.
Whether egotism or genius motivates me,
I can't help exposing its basic elements
To anyone who approaches — anybody at all —
As though friend and foe own my soul.

Curious, this familiar anonymity. Or is it?
Perhaps my poetry fills the silhouette
College students describe
Deftly reciting any of my many classic verses
And plagiarizing them when, first learning to write,
They evoke my rhythmic, mellifluous measures;
Their emulation is my delusion's reincarnation.

All my adult life, I've experimented with disguises
By which I might transcend silence,
Arrest, suspend, nullify the sentence
Imposed on me before my earthly birth,
Decreeing me ineligible for fleshly consolation,
Mandating my existence depend on fantasy,
Invention, and dementia instead of passion and love.

Tonight, sitting alone in distant Oxford,
Sipping Soave Bolla, I miss my children,
My house, sleeping in my own bed,
An echo my dreams might remember and occupy
As they once did when youthful fire guided me
And my ambitious mind seeded carefree metaphors,
Pro-created holistic tropes.

Now, loneliness and despondency overwhelm my heart;
It weakens, slows, implodes.
I can't fathom what has brought me back
To this tempting desolation, unless . . .
Unless Fate itself has contracted with me
To attempt my mortal redemption.
Disoriented, I run naked under Mississippi's moon.

Chapter Two
DELTA PASSAGES

Blown off Course

Cruise control engaged,
Radar, sonar, sporadic radio static
Suffusing my hemispheres as I sail south
Past Luxora, Victoria, and Osceola
Under a tornado-angry sky,

I begin to quiver and twitch
As if every nerve were a halyard
Drawn typhoon-taut,
Poised to deliver a massive whiplash
To my sparrow's heart.

A sharp-edged lightning barb
Burns a permanent scar into my cornea,
Startles me out of drowsiness.
My ship drifts leeward
Into the murky waves buffeting sea lanes

Then returns to its channel
As though by ghostly intervention.
Intermittent rain intensifies,
Transforms into a continuous deluge,
Shreds my sheets like shot pocking Yankee flags.

For the next half hour,
My vessel remains inextricably fixed
In an oil tanker's backwashing draft.
Unable to pass for waterlogged vision,
My lungs breathe its diesel reek,

Fight to prevent asphyxiation
By sending my brain after lunatic hallucinations.
Lepanto, Jericho, West Memphis flicker,
Retreat phosphorescently.
Now, without reason, I head westerly

Toward Hughes, Marianna, Forrest City,
Neither escaping nor embracing demons,
Rather off course, washed overboard,
Lost at sea, gasping, about to drown:
Ishmael, up to his neck in misdirection.

Working the Promised Land

Down I-55,
Having reached the Marion junction,
Just miles north of West Memphis,
I turn right, westerly,
Onto Highway 40, then proceed cautiously
Sixteen miles to the Hughes turnoff,
Where my disappearance begins.

Traversing one side of the triangle
Connecting me with Forrest City and Marianna,
Rain diminishing to a drizzle, I squint,
More from shame than eyestrain,
Glimpsing hovels, canted and ramshackle,
That might be hencoops
Hammered together in a hurricane

Rather than houses twenty by twenty feet,
Made with odds and ends
Gathered by resourceful tenants
To accommodate their paltry needs:
The South's neo-cubist and -dadaist movements
Adapted to the living soul's *nada*-body.
Suddenly I pass Greasy Corners,

Population 24, then enter Hughes
And stop to buy a bag of Brach's lemon drops
At Lock's Food Center,
Which squats innocuously at road's edge
Like the town's one cop behind it,
Poised to give kangaroo-court tickets.
Close by, the high-school band

Adds insult to the injurious air
Practicing for Friday night's football game.
Just outside of town, a paving crew,
All blacks save its supervisor,
Tries to revive tired shoulders.
I slow, obeying raised or lowered red flags;
Resigned eyes remark my air-conditioned insularity

With stares generations wide.
Something primordial about the land frightens me,
Intensifies my uneasiness.
Perhaps it's the somnolence of growing things,
Their lackadaisical silence,
That loudly reminds me
Time keeps a completely different beat down here:

It's always premature or much too late;
Everything in between is crawlspace.
Maybe it's just that cotton and soybeans
Refuse to be slaves to a clock or a season.
Whatever, I sense myself captive,
A tenant in this hellish Delta,
A migrant poet out of his element,

Forced to interlope in territories
Where metaphors are ripe for the picking.
Soon I'll arrive in West Helena,
Work both sides of Poverty's furrows,
Stay the night in a bug-infested motel,
Then strike out for new fields —
Next time, Mississippi!

In Flood Time

Crossing the bridge at Helena, Arkansas,
I see beneath me
The soggy blotter it spans
Oozing perniciously beyond its banks
As if someone has spilled into its channel
An entire sky of inky nightmares.

For wide miles,
Fields bordering Old Man glisten;
Water stands ubiquitously in creeks, gullies,
And culverts; last year's furrows
Are finger-paint smears
On the murky Delta's unearthly surface.

This mid-April, the mid-South
Is no place to be contemplating planting;
Its saturated flatness rejects the notion
With seditious viciousness.
The cloaca below me refuses to absorb and funnel
One more sedimentary ton.

And as I drive toward Clarksdale, Mississippi,
Turn easterly for Oxford,
I realize that the land,
Like its vassals and lords,
Hasn't a chance at either succeeding or failing
By its own plan or hand.

It, they, must accept their fate and pray
And wait for May, when, by God's grace
(Not without grave consequences),
Irrigation will have scratched its sepia signature
Across the face of Everyman's deed,
Marking all old liens PAID.

Passing through this extended bayou,
I'm reminded of the Mariner drowning in thirst;
Here, a similar paradox obtains:
Earth, earth, everywhere earth,
And not a clod to turn!
Worse, flash flooding curses today's forecast.

Abnegating Fate

I view this rain-gray Delta day
As if through a handkerchief:
Oncoming vehicles slide out of and into focus
Like goldfish in a murky pool;
Their headlights are fear-filled eyes
Peering from a moonlit cypress swamp.

On both sides of the highway I take
From West Helena to Oxford,
Defunct gins, soggy fields,
And cotton stalks, waving unpicked tufts
Like tattered truce flags,
Appropriate the remaining daylight,

Making my journey an inward search
To the heart of a glacier
Whose whiteness drives men berserk.
As I go, the opening slowly closes;
Twilight changes to groping,
Groping to total surrender.

I pull off onto a stony shoulder
To pass the hours dozing
Between hallucinatory interludes.
All-night trucks spraying water
Shiver my bones with primitive moaning,
Capsize what few peaceful dreams I have.

Morning never arrives;
Instead, a translucent shimmer enshrouds me.
Dawn is sleep's yawn.
I stretch, resume my travels
As though rain never detained me
Nor fog caused me to fantasize my own funeral.

May Stocktaking

Snakes prematurely dispossessed of their nests;
Levees tested; fire ants on the loose;
Fields backed up like clogged sewers
With viscous silt and sludge;
Entire commercial districts desolate on Saturday:

The mid-South winces under such oppressiveness.
About the only businesses flourishing
Are fishing with crickets and minnows
On crooked bamboo poles
And church with an emphatic Baptist persuasion.

All other preoccupations, professions, and hobbies
Take secondary and tertiary places
In this season-oriented civilization,
Where livelihood and survival alike are measured
In bushels or bales per acre and inches of rain.

Still, despite modern suppressive techniques,
The land's most exportable commodity remains Bigotry;
Neither cotton nor soybeans can encroach,
Supplant its hold over a market
Dominated by "traditional Christian values and morality."

Not even herpes, hookworm, kudzu,
Carcinogens drifting down from crop dusters,
Food stamps, taxes, boll weevils,
Nor losing the Civil War
Is considered as abject as black skin.

One "African-American" generation after another
Is born mortgaged, foreclosed, repossessed,
Auctioned into Egypt.
Emancipation crawls on hands and knees
Toward St. Louis, Chicago, Boston,

But it hasn't even reached Helena, Clarksdale,
Marks, Ruleville, Hughes, Soudan, or Memphis.
Although June planting, July growth,
And August harvest cancel all debts,
Blur distinctions through September's end,

Whites eventually reinvent God's Covenant,
Interpret Scripture to exculpate themselves,
Blame society's ills on the Ethiope.
This May, the earth seems oddly dismayed,
As though Noah's rains might not abate.

Inundation

This Sunday on which I've left West Helena,
Heading for Oxford,
Registers May's midpoint.
Such lush puberty arouses my eyes:
Magnolia, spirea, weeping willow,
Anomalies so green
One might never suspect
The weird stirrings at their submerged feet.

But the fields are turbulent,
Many of them murky oceans and seas
After recent flash floods.
Even undulant acres of rice are incontinent
And unable to germinate seeds.
One more storm and the entire Delta
May dissolve into primordial swampland
Fit for wading diplodocuses and stegosaurs.

Driving at a snail's pace,
I see trailers, tractors, churches, shacks
Floating on the earth's surface
Like toys in a bathtub's stagnant water.
I pass Clarksdale, Marks, Batesville,
Reach I-55, then continue easterly over Highway 6,
Trying to let forgetting dry my memory,
But this inundation persists.

How curious to witness this region
So glutted with flooding
One could almost fish it with a bamboo pole,
Especially when I can still envision
These same lands craving rain
On their wrinkled bellies just last August,
Drawing up beneath the scald
Like slugs sprinkled sadistically with salt.

Commuting over the Wilderness Route

From Smitty's, just off the Square,
The hub, I exit Oxford,
Unceremoniously following South Lamar —
Silk Stocking Avenue —
Past floating steamboat-gothic ghosts,
Then out onto Highway 6, heading due west
Towards Clarksdale, and Helena, Arkansas.

Neither the gray day nor its rain
Diminishes my urgency to escape;
They create a dialogue
The miles articulate
As May's storm-torn desolation
Awakens me to pervasive stagnation
Without and within my brain's mid-South:

Silent, seasonally defunct gin companies
Surrounded by cotton cages
Stuck in mud like winos in gutters;
Implement dealers, their lots glutted
With factory-new Case tractors, Deere pickers;
Motels crying like desperate Loreleis
To every stray salesman passing by;

White "public" academies, privately funded
To avoid the Supreme Court's ukase, to integrate,
And let the races continue to be educated
Equal-yet-separate;
Spayed fields, anonymous as graves hastily dug
By retreating armies. Just recording it all
Gives me fits, disturbs equanimity.

Lafayette, Panola, and Quitman counties
List and sink behind me
Like torpedoed ships in the wartime Pacific.
Soon I'm traveling north on 61,
Through Coahoma County, on a rutted Delta road
Paralleling Old Man,
Being passed by everyone this nasty morning.

I neither know nor care why I'm escaping,
Let alone from what, to whom.
My actions are my passport;
Their itinerary varies from weather to whether,
Depending on inimical Fate's dimmest whim.
Today's mission is to avoid disappearing,
Emptiness the heart's destination.

West Helena's West Side

Abruptly, I exit Highway 49 onto North Baringo
To explore the West Side's auricle.
I, with Missouri license plates,
Fancy, late-model station wagon
Gleaming red as a spit-shined fire engine,
Make myself conspicuous cruising too slowly
As though gawking at casualties in a ten-car pileup.
All eyes peer in at me, peer in,
Leering at the anomalous creature I've become:
Captive Gulliver in Lilliput.
They're a gregarious breed,
These inhabitants of West Helena's "Shantyville":
Children, whose toys are each other,
Garbed in torn shorts and shirts, barefoot;
The girls with cornrowed coifs,
Their rowdy counterparts close-cropped, nappy,
Playing jump rope, swat-the-pebble,
Whose trophies are smiles and laughter;

The women socializing like parakeets and cockatiels
Set free in a pet store,
Gossiping from shack to hovel, porch to front door,
In their rickrack canvassing
From "cain see to cain't see";
The men, youthful and aged,
Sedentary as sedated circus tigers,
Jocularly squabbling, almost falling asleep
Between drawled dialogues, all oblivious
Of the highway's squall paralleling their interplay.
This enclave, whose combined per capita income
Might equal that of one middle-class Memphis family,
Has an integrity paradoxically assured
By its very poverty,
A shoddiness so long endured,
Whose symbols are tumble-down stoops,
Drooping, corrugated tin roofs,
Yards strewn with rusted cars,

Gamecocks and guinea hens, worn-out tires,
Fires spewing gaseous effluvia every season,
Even in 100-degree heat,
That no one thinks of anyone else
As a disgrace to the neighborhood, the community,
Not keeping pace with local gentry.
Even the two churches, profoundly Baptist,
Leave everything to be desired for appearance's sake;
They are indistinguishable from the grocery store
And barbecue stand three doors up from it.
This area, no more than ten square blocks,
These blacks, so closely interwoven,
Provide me no sociological microcosm
Or demographic cross section.
My mind takes no consolation
From drawing easy academic conclusions
To deny or neutralize their existence;
Instead, I feel compassion for them.

Five minutes protract into five years
As I weave up and down the potholed streets,
Lost in a maze, befuddled, anxious
Despite the colossal docility pervading this place,
Trying to locate an opening, escape.
Black babies, teenagers, women and men,
Fat, emaciated, tattered, happy-go-lucky,
Flash past me
Like silhouettes on a praxinoscope reel;
I seem to be standing still,
Fixed in fluid suspension,
Spinning my wagon's wheels full tilt,
Until, gratuitously, the highway materializes,
Heaving me once again into the speeding milieu
Which refuses to see and acknowledge
West Helena's West Side.
I drive east toward Oxford,
Knowing I won't arrive in my original guise.

Chapter Three
"FREEDOM RIDER"

The Ghost of Schwerner Returns

*Michael Schwerner and Andrew Goodman, two
New York Jews, and James Chaney, a Mississippi
black, were abducted and killed by members of
the Ku Klux Klan in the infamous summer of
1964. None of the perpetrators was ever tried for
murder.*

Unlike the "Yankee jew" "nigger sympathizer"
Who used to pass down this pine-lined stretch
Between Memphis and Oxford
Yelling obscenities at imaginary rednecks
From the sanctuary of his speeding station wagon,
Practicing inflammatory speeches
Citing abolitionist tracts
Tracing the genealogy of Southern inhumanity
Back to slave days,
I return this frigid, sunny afternoon
Without any hint of the old zealousness
That branded me outlander, interloper,
A dissident voice whose phone should be tapped.

Now, invisibled by political irrelevance
In the very territory I yet love and fear,
I slip past Hurricane Creek,
Arkabutla Lake, Como, the Tallahatchie River,
Catch the Batesville exit,
Head east toward Jefferson,
The core of Yoknapatawpha's heart.
I know my contemporaries have evaporated
And that although superficial customs have changed,
Political representation has meliorated,
And integration is taken for granted,
Racial issues are still the toilet paper
"Whitey" uses to wipe his ass.

So why, I wonder with exasperation,
Have I driven south again,
Abandoning my "domestic tranquility"
To provide for the common defense of nobody,
*

Since cries no longer rise like smoke?
Perhaps the answer lies in just remembering,
Not allowing all the dust to settle,
Keeping something stirred, the slightest irritant,
To make the eye weep vicariously,
If not actually — that ineradicable desire
To prevent forgetting from seeding weeds
In my mind's garden, which needs constant tending.
I'm returning today to ask, "Has anything changed?"

Going to a Colloquium at Ole Miss, 1982

A celebration in honor of James Meredith, held twenty years from the day of his being the first black student admitted to the University of Mississippi, September 30, 1962.

Up as far as Hayti and Sikeston,
The northernmost zone for growing cotton,
Crops have already been harvested;
Below West Helena,
Clarksdale, Cleveland, and Greenville,
The lethargic Delta
Is awash with white polka dots:
A late September snow in the lower 90s.

And as I drive, bolls broken wide open,
Overflowing into furrowed rows
Pressing against both sides of the highway,
Remind me of popcorn, in a green dish,
I'd like to snatch with my fingers,
Nibble repeatedly to satiety;
Even as my imagined snack turns back to cotton,
Mississippi's salt stings my lips.

Suddenly, each fluffy puff,
Drooping innocuously, becomes a Klansman
Beneath a sheet amidst leafy coverts.
With paranoiac misgivings,
I increase speed, aim eastward,
Hoping to elude this White Citizens' Council,
Reach Oxford intact, in time to witness
James Meredith dictate black supremacy.

Chance Encounter

Last evening, in Fulton Chapel,
On the Ole Miss campus,
Filled to capacity with blacks and whites
And national news media
Brandishing video equipment
Instead of the National Guard bearing M-1's,
Night sticks, and tear-gas canisters,
I witnessed History's nearly complete demise:

A score of years rolled up behind a podium
In the guise of a retiring, paunchy figure
Of the student youth who, at twenty-nine,
Defied an entire society
Entrenched in its White Citizens' Councils;
A bewhiskered man chanting in damning staccato,
Not strident yet uncompromising
In his desire to effect black reunification in Africa,

Basic rights, elemental decencies still ignored,
According to his heart,
At Ole Miss and in America,
And to stanch the rampant abnegation of equality,
As exemplified by ratios, facts, statistics,
In every profession across this disfranchised land.
I watched half the audience exit
In a conspicuous flurry as his speech concluded,

The predominantly white dispersion
Not even lingering to hiss him off the stage,
Their flight disappointment's overt manifestation.
They'd come, I suspect,
Like spectators to a cockfight,
Anticipating blood.
Even as I listened, I couldn't help wondering
What he was doing these days . . . Meredith,

Whose education had entitled him to life's riches;
Why, living in Jackson
For decades in uncontroversial seclusion,
He'd satisfied himself owning a bar and tree farm,
Taken a second wife,
Begun a family once again
Instead of assuming a more active role in civil rights.
Not that I faulted him —

I sympathized with his acquiescence to the establishment
In a state singularly deplorable for its poverty.
Nonetheless, I grew sad
Seeing this innocuous soul, who had asserted himself
With such courage in 1962
For the sake of abjuring second-class citizenship.
And as I watched and listened,
My eyes and throat choked with invisible grief.

Later, in the lobby of the Alumni House,
Where we were staying,
I shyly introduced myself,
Explained my presumptuousness
By describing how he'd spoken for me in those days
When we were of college age,
That my admiration for his actions at that time
Persisted yet.

I was glad for the chance to tell him so,
Though both of us seemed not anachronistic
But slightly anomalous amidst students
Who'd grown up in integrated schools, never known
(And so regarded all our stories as boring)
The vituperations of Ross Barnett,
Orval Faubus, James Eastland, George Wallace,
And their legions of anonymous, cowardly followers.

As we exhausted our small talk,
I handed him my copy of *Three Years in Mississippi*
And asked if he'd inscribe his book to me.
Once back in my room, alone,
Reading his note in oversized script —
"To Our Future /
J.H. Meredith / Sept 30, 1982" —
I realized *our* future was already history.

Implacable Impasse

So strange! It's so strange
How so little has changed so much
In so many ways
Nobody can touch these days
Or expose with a divining rod's twin tines,
Intellect and Emotion.
Twenty years have elapsed,
Yet black students at Ole Miss
Maintain that ingrained low profile
No amount of administrative rhetoric and cant
Proclaiming "affirmative action"
Can elevate from the old Colonial tyrannies
Handed down not an eye for an eye
But inequity for iniquity, bigotry for welt.

Sad! It's so terribly tragic
To see white coeds and their cotillion beaus
Coming and going, fumbling and stumbling
In numb paroxysms of drunken passion
Neither will remember forever after,
Unable to quote the "Michelangelo poet"
Or even recall the trauma of both '62s:
Neither Shiloh nor Meredith
Fits their neat schemes for law school,
Positioned riches, political recognition.
Chauvinism and Faulknerian binges
Pose no radical threat to their success;
Fancy clothes, flashy cars, faddish cosmetics,
And cash-cow sugar daddies even less.

Refusing to let their hearts intermarry,
Both heritages lose uniqueness.
Homogeneity is the creature incest begets.

Legacies

Shiloh, Corinth, Brices Cross Roads
Echo in my veins as I flee Oxford
And head for Missouri. Once more,
Those names resonate out of an old order
Yet proclaimed preeminent
By every Ole Miss Bubba Reb in polo shirt
And rouge-cheeked, magnolia-perfumed coed
Sporting designer blouse and shorts.

They parade before me like brigades
Practicing to enter a fracas
Only days, histories away: handsome law students,
Elegantly mannered, soft-spoken belles-to-be,
Whose greatest efforts will be spent
In defense of spendthrift sentiments, divorces,
Penchants for Kentucky bourbon, Russian vodka,
Mexican tequila, Mississippi white lightnin'.

Even now, through Tennessee and into Arkansas,
I both lament and envy the generations
Past and present whose heritage —
Whatever skeletons rattle in their closets
Like swords clattering in rusty scabbards —
Cements them, despite primal fear of the future,
To a sense of place.
I have only myself to claim and blame!

Street Cleaner

I maneuver through downtown Farmington,
All six blocks,
Briefly amused by an Elgin street cleaner
Shifting frenziedly from curb to curb
Like an overturned stag beetle
Straining to right itself.
For all twenty-two miles over 32 to I-55,
I can't eradicate its persistent image;
Each cow, tractor, and barn
Rushes at me, jerking from side to side,
Belly-brushes whisking me under.

Although for an hour or so,
Going south toward Cape Girardeau,
Sikeston, New Madrid, Hayti,
I fantasize my own potential victimization
By diabolical forces,
Becoming gratuitous human detritus
Beneath an infernal machine controlled from Below,
And despite my visceral uneasiness,
Most likely from too much coffee
Or maybe because of my destination,
I know my real fears stem from loneliness.

Mist lifts in vaporous ray-streams
As if sipped through straws by a thirst-crazed sun.
Unnoticed, I traverse Missouri, Arkansas, Tennessee,
Then enter Mississippi
And apply for an operator's license
At the Benevolent Klavern of White Pariahs.
Suddenly I'm guiding the Elgin
North and south along Lamar,
Trying, against the bias, to sweep bigotry
From Oxford's one-way streets;
But they're too dirty, and my tanks are bone-dry.

Ghost Writer

The rains complain, they groan;
Their moaning pervades this evening
Like a venerative threnody
Spoken over the grave of an old friend
While, indoors at The Warehouse,
William Styron and Willie Morris stroke the Muse's lute,
Take decorum to new heights
Of art and charm.
The town's dilettantes, perched around their table,
Flutter in such august midst,
Preen, and trip over unpracticed pretensions
To literary insight and discipline.

In a corner booth by myself, sipping wine,
Peeling and nibbling beer-boiled shrimp,
Trying to write poetry in my trusty ledger,
I maintain a low profile,
Consider myself an outsider
Invited by a simple slip of the tongue
Whispered by the lissome ghost of William Faulkner,
Flying earthward earlier this afternoon.
I know all these people by name,
Yet they don't see me;
Paradoxically,
My heart is Ellison's invisible white counterpart.

Strangulation

Kudzu is a radical manifestation
My imagination can't eradicate
No matter how concentrated my gaze inward.
In every direction,
I see green-seething Piranesian chains,
Sense their impending threat
As I drive westerly out of Oxford
Into a wet morning fog.

Suddenly, vision is engulfed, extinguished.
I strain to maintain the median
Between my eyes and brain.
By degrees, ubiquitous loblolly pine trees,
Embedded in red clay,
Absorb me, admit me into their keeping
As though the kudzu were a freshly dug grave
Into which my spirit has just descended.

Ku Klux Kudzu

As I drive out of Oxford toward I-55,
Two blatant paradoxes, like Medusa-snakes,
Coil about my barely awake brain
And squeeze my imagination to painful hyperventilation.
The first, steeped in irony, materializes,
Separates into a pair of black college girls
Walking briskly against my flight;
Sporting bright-red T-shirts
Proclaiming "Ole Miss Rebels,"
Both, I suppose, in plain sight on this public highway,
Consider themselves immune to violation.

And as I go,
This summer day's other pervasive presence, kudzu,
Sends out its seething tendrils
And juicy leaves to take up accommodations
In my otherwise vacant psyche's eyes.
Strewn in festoons and cascading green drapes
From treetops to earth,
It resembles stalactitic tunnels and chambers
Perforating labyrinthine caves
Through whose voluptuous illusions
My gaze passes in hypnotized fascination.

Abruptly, kudzu and T-shirts fuse, dissolve,
Green and red assuming confusing hues
Without contrast beneath the mist-sifting sun
As Mississippi becomes Tennessee,
Then Arkansas, then southeast Missouri,
And I'm home, almost deleted of memory's legacies,
Almost assimilated again into my 1950s,
Neoconservative dream of Suburban Utopia,
Whose prosperity would mediate all evils,
Milk dry my hallucinations' venomous threats
If not defang their bites.

But right now, safe in my house,
I can still see that kudzu
Stalking those black girls wearing red "Rebels" shirts,
*

Walking nonchalantly from Sardis toward Oxford
To partake of Saturday shopping,
Still hear it hissing as it uncoils, slithers,
Stretches to catch their apparently carefree spirits,
Transmogrify them into mummy-trees,
Whose blight, disguised as subtle beauty,
Will nurture the procession of retrogressive evolution,
And I realize I never left Mississippi alive.

Chapter Four

INTIMATIONS OF FAULKNER

Admiration for a Man Who Admired Faulkner

For Professor James W. Webb

Decay infiltrates my nostrils,
That pervasive reek of cancerous flesh
Being eaten from the inside out.
I wince, gasp for precious breath
While trying to perpetuate amenities,
Not stifle conversation about chief surgeons,
Catheters, chemotherapy, radiation.
My replies die in their own choking silence.

On initially visiting Oxford eight years ago,
We stopped first to meet him.
Then, the house and porch
Were antiseptic, pristine, and quaint.
He, at that time, curator of Rowan Oak,
Spoke anecdotally of his famous former neighbor.
His wife applauded his recitation;
We were enchanted. It was all so spotless.

Now, I squirm as his wife applauds medical anecdotes
She's heard three dozen times recently,
Refusing to intrude and factualize
A piece of intended truth the drugs distort
Or to cue a forgotten line or two.
The screens are pushed out, curtains torn;
Dust has thickly accumulated.
A shabby pallor invests the house with gloom.

That first trip, my wife and I were untainted too
With our beautiful six-month-old girl.
They delighted so
Knowing we'd journeyed such a distance
To share and appreciate their heritage
By exploring their hero's domain.
He reveled in showing us Rowan Oak
As though he owned it himself.

Before I go,
He leads me back to the converted bedroom
That houses books, files, artifacts:
His thirty-five years of academic desiderata.
I pause before his most treasured possession,
A framed photograph of William Faulkner,
Recite the inscription on its mat
Which the author penned to him in his minuscule script.

* * *

Two days ago,
I received word from a friend at Ole Miss
That he had died two weeks prior.
Even now, I see him inviting us in eight years ago,
My wife and child and me,
Mere strangers in that moment only,
And I cry for the man I grew to admire
Not just for revering the writer I've also admired.

Jason's Plaint

"Once a bitch, always a bitch!"
I says about days like this,
Hotter than blazes, even for Jefferson.
Jesus, when sweat starts beading up on your face
Heavier than a lathered racehorse
Without so much as moving in your seat
Reaching for a chaw of tobacco,
Something's all out of whack!
Believe it or not, it's those New York jews
Doing their insider trades,
Leveraging the entire commodities market
From New Orleans through Memphis to Wall Street.
I still ain't exactly figured out
How they create these outrageous droughts,
But sure as hell, I tell you,
Those rich kikes can maneuver and manipulate anything,
Including tides, the moon, mulattoes, and octoroons.

But I ain't so stupid as folks 'round here got me pegged.
I'm gonna stick a chunk of Quentin's money
From the little trunk upstairs
Into next-July beans and -August cotton,
Then make a killing — "Nothin' ventured,
Nothin' gained!" I always says.
Hey, wait just one goddamn moment!
What's going on here? Where's *my* savings?
Damn that bitch! She's prized it open,
Stolen the whole shittin' stash of Caddy's cash!
I'll fix her ass but real good!
Just let me catch that slatternly little wench!
"Quentin!" I shout down the hall. "Quentin!"
My words are land mines that detonate inside my head
Every time my tongue trips over that sleazy bitch's name.
"Quentin! Quentin!" I scream, wincing
Until my eyes fill with tears from the sheer pain.

I'll find her ass if I have to drive five counties!
She ain't gonna make a fool outta Jason Compson,
The one remaining sane human being
In a whole barrel of rotten eggs. No sirree!
I'll give her a lickin' like she's never had,
So bad she'll wish my sister, that whore,
Never did born her into this family!
Hey, wait! What's with these tires?
All four flat! Why, that scurrilous bastard!
Well, like I says, "Easy come, easy go!"
I got to take me a passel of aspirins quick,
Before my forehead explodes. Goddamn everything!
This family! This drought! This stinking South!
Why'd I have to inherit such foul luck?
Fuck Fate, women, greedy eastern jew-bait!
I hate it, hate it! Then again,
I reckon I coulda been Quentin or Ben!

Faulkner's Ravished Brides of Quietness

Meta, Ruth, Joan, Else, Jean,
Parenthesized collectively by Estelle.
He needed them,
Each in her disordered place
Within his graceless, inebriated middle-aging,
Who, moving through endless dispassions
He created and embellished for himself
When sidetracked by bills, wills, movie scripts,
Backaches, blackouts, lost pages,
Nonetheless kept the fictive lock stitch
From completely unraveling,
Ultimately wearing, sharing with Estelle
The same tattered fabric they'd cut and sewn
From dream-patterns they'd drafted as teenagers
And would lie buried beneath in St. Peter's.

He needed them to slake the solitude
His demon-laced sullenness
Imposed outwardly from within frontiers
He never fully tamed,
Briefly claiming fragments of landscapes
Contiguous to human desolations,
His brooding moods their lone proprietor.
He needed them to allow him freedom
To expose his deeply disguised gentleness,
Which helped him approximate Love's romantic obbligatos,
Its ever-shifting simulacra
He may have imbibed from verse old and nascent —
"The Phoenix and the Turtle," "Ode on a Grecian Urn,"
A Shropshire Lad, and *Pomes Penyeach* —
Under the stern, possessive coercion of Phil Stone.

He needed these ladies
To teach him how to kiss his Muse's soft hands, toes,
Lips, breasts, sweet, close-cropped cunt,
Which he likened to the Delta,
To show him how to hold Time's quicksilver sands,
Control those wildly ephemeral moments
*

When poetry and prose would rapidly fuse,
Then slowly come undone
In the most wondrous sundering of flesh and emotion:
Two sets of bones directed heavenward
Like Gaudí's *Familia Sagrada* spires.
He needed them, each individually, as lovers,
Quintessences of pedestaled Greek goddesses,
Daughter and Mother at once,
Enthroned in a kind of blessed incestuousness

He alone could justify without excusing
As sole owner of his soul's Holy Roman Empire,
Existing in a timeless sequestration
Transfiguring mother/wife/mistress
Into living visions, real dreams,
By grafting his rib onto motley skeletons,
Trusting passion would fuse the natural seams.
He needed them not as female embodiments,
Androgynous anodynes, but secret sharers
In the outsized genius he'd been bequeathed,
That they might let him forget, occasionally,
Pestiferous sibilances of green horseflies
Dive-bombing the landfill
Behind the Benjy-fence his sense of privacy built
To keep prying eyes from defiling his dominion.

He needed them to remind him, at times,
How sublimely he might aspire
To freeing those two amorous prisoners on the Urn,
Recasting them in eternal embrace,
In God's imagination, anyway,
Before breaking the mold,
Taking the brittle shards with him to the grave,
Where dust makes no distinctions.

Byhalia

What a strange name, Byhalia!
It trips off my tongue's tip
Like those of so many other Mississippi towns,
But it has a significantly different pitch.
I have visited this remote limbo,
Where Faulkner and Death fought one last battle,
To etch on my memory's silver-nitrate plates
His ultimate humiliation,
Experience this Pandemonium firsthand,
No matter that I've arrived
More than twenty years after his pathetic demise,
About which the public knows absolutely *nada*
Beyond the Blotner/Minter/Oates melodrama
It's been bequeathed, despite the "dirty laundry,"
To lullaby its voyeuristic intellect's sleep
From anonymous time to time anon.

I know, though.
I've traveled here, investigated,
Scrutinized the now-defunct Christian Academy,
Whose flaking paint, cubicles, and desolate purlieus
Can't disguise the original sanitarium
Dr. Wright administrated with a stern eye
And his penchant for paraldehyde.
I've interviewed, informally of course,
Relics and derelicts the town has preserved,
Who remember twenty-some years later
The weird *son et lumière* effects
Emanating nightly from that drying-out place,
Where Cousin Jimmy brought Brother Will
For the last time and from whose now-razed gates
Its most celebrated "inmate" escaped,
Then died in a ditch, stark naked.

Purposely, I've driven here from Memphis
To sate curiosity's needs,
Enforce Imagination's mandate
That, eventually, facts must rise above myths
*

And fictions fall by the wayside
Like Mr. Bill himself,
Who refused to be confined like a laboratory rat
In a Skinner-box "drunk tank,"
Opted instead to die in the dust like Vardaman's fish,
"Cooked and et, cooked and et,"
Anonymous as an unsigned Elizabethan sonnet
Consigned to immortality
In an anthology of Renaissance poets,
Speculatively attributed to another Bill, Shakespeare,
With whose brilliance, coincidentally,
His own genius would be equated.

I've journeyed to this northern Mississippi site
To confirm the building really exists,
Where he'd been sentenced to solitary confinement,
Bedridden for days, weeks,
Gradually detoxed so frequently before that fatal visit;
I've ventured here to empathize with his isolation,
Resist believing that his creative juices
Could ever have surrendered to such shabby limitations
Even in his alcoholic stupors and binges,
In which he'd sully himself with his own shit.
Despite those forced marches to Byhalia
Preceding his final one in early July '62,
He obviously knew the "Snopes Trilogy" *had* to be finished,
The Reivers reminisced into existence
Before he could submit to that dread enemy, Destitution;
He couldn't quit before Destiny ditched him.

Tours de Force

From Jefferson, Mississippi,
The reverse-threaded nut
At the hub of Yoknapatawpha's Catherine wheel,
They flow outward,
Along its spokes, toward the earth's rim

And over, just as they first arrived,
Ferried back privately
To Time's origin
On emotion emanating yet from his fictive abyss,
Which, with mere words, he formed into a mythical Cosmos.

Hitched to their own mystic spirit's team,
His people return to truths
Whose actions, accents, dialects, and drawls
Recall their paltry genealogies,
Groping inhabitants of Lascaux's caves:

Benjy holding a broken narcissus;
Joe Christmas grasping his castrated groin;
Henry Armstid lamenting his bolted spotted pony;
Vardaman dragging a fish in the dust
By his mother's umbilicus;

Ike riding the hunt wagon into manhood;
Rider grieving over his knifed wife,
Jackson Fentry for a son he never fathered
Yet loved like his own blood,
Untimely ripped from him by Satan's brothers;

Homer Barron, superintendent of roads,
Courting his own ghost in an open surrey.
These and so many others,
Hypnotic illusions moving in fluid arrest —
Posterity's stroboscopic effect.

Chapter Five

THE SAHARA OF THE BOZART

Faulkner and Yoknapatawpha Conference, 1979

For: Jim Carothers
Tom McHaney
Michael Millgate
Noel Polk
Jim Watson
Judy Wittenberg

This return journey is especially empty,
Whose inconspicuous exit from Oxford
Was accomplished, like its arrival,
In total aloneness.
I grieve on taking to the road again.

Disoriented, deprived of camaraderie,
Which, during the week just dissolved,
Grew like twining ivy
Out of fertile, disparate minds
United by a sublimely common passion,

I grieve over constant dislocations
That shape my clay into unfinished pieces —
Michelangelo's "Slaves."
The frequent rearranging of my soul
Has rendered memory prone to forgetting faces,

Gentle sensibilities, intellectual distillations,
Molded out of silence and darkness,
Waiting to reach my ears and eyes,
My entire inspired vitality.
I grieve for affection left in friends' safekeeping,

Not certain when, if ever again,
We'll reconvene
To feast from a common table,
Set our hearts in synchronous wonderment,
Touch the source of Youth's musical exuberance.

I can only surmise from our reluctance to part,
Our inchoate, overt remorse
On witnessing our rosary unbead a sigh at a time,
That joy is infinite,
Dying a mere detail

The mind delegates to corporeal subordinates.
I weep as my body flies homeward
Through quietude suffused with epiphanies,
Knowing that our laughter, happiness, and friendship
Must desert us as we return to ourselves.

Innisfree, Mississippi, 1983

This fall morning, I depart Oxford,
Heading not home but south,
Via back roads,
Past Water Valley, Coffeeville, to I-55,
Then down toward Jackson,
Where, for two days, I'll assimilate rhetoric,
Casuistry fashioned by and for professors
Who teach English or law,
Only dream of writing or trying cases,

At a very high-class Conference
(With a very uppercase "C," I might add)
Calculated to promulgate harmony
Between different disciplines,
Whose main theme is (can you imagine?)
"The Law in Faulkner's Fiction."
How else might Mississippi
Expect to attract pedagogues from Johns Hopkins,
Harvard, U. of Chicago?

Skimming Yalobusha County's
Autumnally hued, kudzu-cascading woods
This tranquil Saturday a.m.
Distracts me from my actual destination;
Ripe, white-tufted plants in fields
Are angels' hands waving from teeming depots
As my express traverses Eden,
Edging toward the pedigreed citadel.
For an instant, an eon, I'm untainted again.

Out of My Element

Driving apprehensively,
I penetrate to the center of the state
Like a medieval surgeon jamming a trepan
Into the brain's fluid core.

Not sure what I'll discover,
I press down I-55 toward Jackson,
Chanting Mississippi's mantra of demagogues:
Bilbo, Barnett, Vardaman.

Suddenly, the sun plummets into my rearview mirror
Like a buffalo tricked over a precipice;
Oncoming headlights
Announce the day's funeral procession.

Gray eyes inside the stampeding sky
Scrutinize my unyielding shadow,
Undress me with their passionless stares;
Auschwitz-still, I prepare for rain showers

While Gloom's ruffled buzzard
Hovers above my ragged, steaming shape.
I shudder for having agreed to attend a lecture
On "Legal, Racial, and Moral Codes

In *Go Down, Moses* and the 'Snopes Trilogy,'"
Especially since I'm a poet at heart
Who reads Faulkner just to get intoxicated,
Not aid and abet pedagogy.

Faulkner and Yoknapatawpha Conference, 1988

Arriving after 6:00 this Sunday,
In time to catch sunset on the run,
I park my car, check into the Alumni House
(Room 124 — Faulkner's old P.O. box number),
Change into jogging shorts,
Enter Mississippi's merciless heat,
And make the ritualistic circle
I've taken on returning to Oxford
Nine years in a row:
From my motel on the Ole Miss campus,
Through the Grove, around the Lyceum and library,
Over the tracks, up University Avenue
Toward South Lamar, north into town,
Around the Lafayette County Courthouse,
Which Faulkner dubbed "the hub,"
Then back up Lamar, west on Old Taylor Road,
Finishing at Rowan Oak.
My mythic Olympian trek
Signaling the week's activities have officially begun,
I can now unpack my bags and settle in.

Once again, another conference will,
As it always has, overrun Yoknapatawpha
With didacticism and academic claptrap
About the writer who's no longer around
To defend himself against his adversary,
Dilettantism,
The hydra-like chimera he hated and feared,
That best friend of the NAACP —
National Academy for the Advancement of Cultural Pedantry.
When the week ends, if all goes as planned,
Every attendee will understand more about the man
Who penned *Absalom, Absalom!*
Than Thomas Sutpen, Rosa Coldfield, and Quentin Compson
Could ever possibly infer
By deciphering from the words
Beneath whose surfaces they reside
*

His whisperous, cryptic intellect's implications.
And after they've all left,
I'll jog once more around the Courthouse
And nod to Faulkner in knowing disgust.

Trying to Survive Monday Morning's Lectures

None of us in this too-fluorescent ballroom
Wears Time's insistence on his wrist identically;
Each of our plastic-crystalled prisms
Catches and projects certain impertinences —
Deconstructionistic and self-reflexive repetitions —
Spoken by Matherish lecturers, distracted from life,
Not to us in the audience
But to those passing just beyond the windows,
Trudging through Mississippi's August firestorm.

Weary from trying to absorb literary criticism
Contrived by hubristic scholars
Faulkner nicknamed "academical gumshoes,"
I attempt to transcend with yawns and daydreams
Their unrelievedly hermetic disquisitions,
Dissociate myself from abstract systems,
Fabrics stitched by intellects
Too solipsistic to compose creative prose,
Coax blue strokes on white ledger sheets into poetry.

Dazed, I lapse into suppressed rage,
Compulsively glancing at the slender hands
Advancing implacably around my watch face
As though, somehow,
I might escape its fix on History's existence
By arresting Time with visionary images
Dimming swimming within my mind's Charles River.
But like Quentin weighted down with sadirons,
I sink beneath their argumentative currents and drown.

Picnic at Rowan Oak

For Jim Carothers

The clipped grounds surrounding Rowan Oak
Seethe like a weary athlete
Beneath Mississippi's deep-breathing humidity.
We drown,
Who have convened this week in Oxford
To pay obeisance to His simulacrum:
Not sweet Jesus, but "Billy" Faulkner,
Conspicuous in his transcendence.

Each clapboard, every joist and floor beam,
Brick, shingle, drainpipe, chimney, and window
Recalls his small footfalls,
His high-pitched, diminished drawl,
As though he, not we, his priesthood,
Were shivering the earth's tympanum in our stirring
And languid carousing about the house
He reclaimed from desolation, tamed, and named.

Ah, but aren't we committing a desecration
By violating this serenity he abdicated in July,
Anno Domini 1962?
Who gave us the right to infiltrate his privacy,
Ordained us trustees of his domain,
That we might partake of his once-vibrant spirit
By picnicking on his lawn, porch,
And in his overgrown formal gardens,

Spawning our own petty narcissisms,
Where once he grieved over Joe Christmas,
Lena Grove, Wash Jones, Benjy, Quentin, and Caddy,
Got pissed off at Sutpen's cavalier excesses,
Ike McCaslin's rigidity, Benbow's garrulity,
Guffawed until the gods themselves seemed shamed
By Cora Tull's outrageous piety,
Reverend Gail Hightower's flatulent eloquence?

Undaunted, we analyze neither our motives nor his;
Instead, we ensconce ourselves
In convenient contradistinctions to each other,
Arrogantly registering our various ambitions,
Noting one another's tedious locations
Within Academe
Or slightly to the left or right of Life,
All of us paltry approximations of his genius

Despite our numerous publications, degrees, our vitae,
Who've come to spend this week in Yoknapatawpha
To observe, listen for whispers,
Discern those certain sublime scents, sounds,
Twilit hues to which he lucidly responded,
Hoping to take back to our sanctuaries
And kinsmen on the peripheries
That inscrutable, illusory Essence,

Proclaim that each of us is similarly gifted,
Has his capacity to create a cosmos
Like constructing a "henhouse in a hurricane."
But the fried chicken is greasy,
And the salad is soggy as seaweed;
The paper cups wilt in our hands like flowers —
A curious eucharist,
Shabby communion with our Lord, "Billy."

Educational Miscegenation

Despite my heart's disinclination,
A gray, shapeless melancholy
Has chased me out of Oxford this afternoon,
Sent me fleeing in such soiled, sullen sadness
Not even familiar road-poetry
Assuages the pervasive one-on-oneness
Disaffecting the two of us, memory and me.

For a week, I've eluded anonymity
Courting approval of students and teachers
Into whose custody I remanded my shadow:
Academicians, mainly, whose motivations,
Fundamentally inimical to mine,
Seemed enemies of freedom and creativity,
Hiding behind their rhetorical, course-titled lives.

Arriving home to an empty bed,
My emptier head vanishes into thin forgetting,
Within whose dense Big Woods
I suddenly recognize my jettisoned soul
As the black bastard child of Roth Edmonds,
White scion of Ike McCaslin's ancestors —
A pariah doomed to endure pedagogical miscegenation.

Chapter Six
ROWAN OAK'S COVERTS

Intimations of Immortality in Spring

For Louis Dollarhide,
whose Of Art and Artists *beguiled me.*

The entire horizon is a green-dripping abstract,
Each bud and node
A broken tube leaving oily smudges
My eyes can almost touch for their fresh impastos.

As I drive south, hour by hour,
The canvas seems to complete its own design
One invisible stroke at a time.
My arrival goes unnoticed for its ghostly halo.

Everything in Oxford is in riot —
Magnolia, oleander, crepe myrtle, verbena, honeysuckle —
Except me; at best,
My conception and execution are yet questionable.

I await a painterly inspiration
To color me into existence,
Locate my place in this green-dripping abstract,
That I might begin setting;

Drying requires such a protracted transition
Between dying and living again.

Ghost House

For Victoria Fielden Johnson

Tourists with time to kill,
Bookish sorts, and the simply curious approach,
Step close, closer, to the porticoed porch,
Pressing their inquisitive faces
Against windows obliquely disclosing stage sets
Once inhabited by real personae,
Not invented poltergeists.

They seem bent on penetrating force fields,
Entering revitalized lives
Silhouetted against scrim shrouds hung from clouds:
Pappy, Estelle, Jill,
Malcolm, Victoria, and Vic-Pic, too,
As well as the ubiquitous blacks, Boojack, Julia,
Uncle Ned, Broadus, Mammy Callie, Andrew Price.

Longing to approximate a sense of place,
Exchange for a pittance of its history
Their entire ordinary existences,
Visitors negotiate mazy shrubs, brick grots,
Follow rotting cedar fence posts
That used to channel spotted Texas ponies
In from the back pasture to Faulkner's penpoint.

Some spend hasty lifetimes,
Others endless afternoons, fixing the illusion.
Most exit mystified, bewitched, few disappointed,
Whose inspirations inspire nothing;
Not a derelict tree, leaking gutter,
Mildewing clapboard, or canting green shutter
Even notices they've come and gone.

Unfazed by their communion-taking crusades,
Holy pilgrimages, retreats, excursions,
His edifice is assimilated inconspicuously
Into Oxford's April twilight.
Mute conduit evermore,
Rowan Oak submits to provoked overgrowth
Reaching up out of Bailey's Woods like a ghost.

Jogging Bailey's Woods

I own this afternoon,
Through whose sultry humidity
My body slips coursing Bailey's Woods.
My winged feet, absorbing jolts,
Compensating for exposed roots
Too old to hold their sandy purchase,
Fall in cosmic cadence —
The mercurial beat that sings the earth alive.

These woods accept my human intrusion,
Intuiting I've come humbly
To offer groans and sweat and pain
Only for the sake of proving
That, despite the bones' brittleness,
The muscles' inflexibility,
My aging spirit can still stave off decay
In plain sight of its skeptical ego.

Soon, Rowan Oak materializes.
I emerge, dripping like a dirge
From a Renaissance cathedral.
Sensibilities spent, my heart explodes;
Its pulse is so loud
Silence can't relinquish its code,
Teach me to translate the bird-chirping
Stirring cedar-deep without violating the solitude.

I cry aloud with relief,
Wipe perspiration from my face,
Clear vision, view the great Greek edifice,
Hoping no one will be home
To accuse me of trespassing,
Tell me I don't belong here
In this vacant southern Delphi.
No windows, doors, or portico columns creak.

No trees whisper. I stalk around the house
Cautiously as a thief about to break and enter,
Caught in its broad-daylight halo
*

Like a moth circling a kerosene lamp,
Shaking out the cramps in my heavy legs
Until dizziness overheats
And feeling ceases. Suddenly I shudder,
Wondering why I've strayed so far from home.

Perhaps lacking adequate humility,
My spirit has brought me to this dappled refuge
To pray that I too — my voice anyway —
Might someday exceed its threshold,
Outshout Faulknerian echoes.
More likely, it's my body demanding equal time,
Requiring trial by fatigue to remind me
I alone own this afternoon, not ghosts.

Waking Sleeping Demons

Having just lunged through Bailey's Woods
On my return path, emerging from its cool coverts
Like a locomotive exiting a tunnel,
I stall, fall to my wobbly knees
Beneath a peach tree teeming with netted bagworms
Suspended in catatonic stupors.

I rise, stare at their airy cocoon,
And blow superheated drafts into it
To excite their swarming dormancy.
Like free-falling parachutists,
They stir, whirl, then unfurl
Until the entire sac is aswirl with nebulae.

All the more for completing a strenuous run
So psychically satisfying
On a Mississippi afternoon this tranquil,
I can't fathom what vagary
Might have motivated me
To commit an act so gratuitous

Or why I should have distracted myself,
No matter how momentarily,
From the elation abating pain begs us celebrate
After spirit and bone fuse earth with sky.
My actions have no precedent;
I've trespassed without provocation.

Spent, yet recovered enough to resume jogging,
I descend again into the womb-woods,
Maneuver toward Rowan Oak,
Hoping, simultaneously, to forget the old,
Discover a new purpose for coming here,
To run free, perfect my humanity,

Practice resurrection in this solitude
By extending my fleshly thresholds.
But, as if whipping my body for apostasy,
The harder I press, the more certain I am
Those squirming worms are Death's earthly surrogates,
Caveats that I must not stop.

Valedictory for a Jogger

For Bob Hamblin,
friend and partner

Occasionally, even familiar locations
Grow indistinct.
Suspended in memory's dense Bailey's Woods,
Energy dissipates, the legs go weak,
The body's best intentions
Betray the brain's sustained demands;
Its nerve-works complain under the overload.

Sunrays slanting across the eyes' screen
In a deep, green haze
Distract focus from the rooted path.
Legs, feet, toes collectively grope
Like a baton straining for an open hand.
Suddenly one foot catches an intractable snag;
Knees buckle;

Earth rushes up to arrest motion,
Appropriate the muscles' shattered hopes.
Pain breaks the tape first.
Utterly defeated, the injured spirit
Curses the Woods' merciless will,
Hobbles home to claim the Timekeeper's trophies:
Ice pack, plaster cast, crutches.

Healed and Back to My Old Pursuits

This predawn Mississippi August a.m.,
It's too steamy even at six
To jog Oxford's streets
Or breathe comfortably walking at a diminished clip.
Steadfastly I fix on magnolias, oaks, and cedars
To resist collapsing from dizziness.

Out of self-preservation,
I seek the shade of Bailey's Woods,
But it's so close in this seething atmosphere
I can almost hear drops from God's clepsydra
Trickling down its myriad flume-shoots;
I listen for moccasins slithering.

There's just no room for humans
Between the humidity's molecules.
Suddenly my eyes behold Rowan Oak,
Looming like a lone, colossal magnolia blossom
Long gone past perfection into drooping putrescence.
I refuse to savor its overripe fragrance,

Choose instead to wait for the right moment
To slip unnoticed through the wide net
Woven of sunrays and shadows,
Back into Imagination's Eden,
Where metaphors and daydreams are Keatsian lovers
Forever chaste, forever chasing each other in urn-circles.

Intimations of Dante at Rowan Oak

For over two decades, until today,
I've tried to transmute desolate scenes,
Routine deeds, mediocre notions, anecdotes,
And my own inadequate spontaneity
Into noble, romantic epics
Through poetry's enchanting medium,
Enhance to mythic dimension
My shabby imagination
By plagiarizing dreams
Redeemed from forgetting by the Mississippi writer
Whose fiction I've admired since college.

For almost twenty-five years, until today,
I've remained suspended in a limbo
Composed of theories not my own,
Committing endlessly convoluted syntax,
Egregiously overreaching my limits,
Eager to make fortuitous discoveries
Like those long-lost Cíbolas, Pharaohs' lairs,
And Dead Sea Scrolls wanderers locate
Every few centuries,
Groping unsuccessfully to penetrate the rose,
Enter the innermost halo,

And be spared the grotesque revelation
That living is no mere exercise in futility
But Futility's slave raised to the third power,
Who bears the Devil's surname, Disillusion.
Sadly, after so many lonely desert treks,
I've emerged this fated afternoon
At the edge of Bailey's Woods,
Where, without daring to draw nearer,
I can sense my hero's ghost
Leaning inebriated from Rowan Oak's balcony,
Screaming, "All hope abandon, ye who enter here!"

Even the Highway Is My Crucifix

Even now, the voracious miles devour the hours,
The hours memory,
On my inexorable exodus northward home.

Oxford, where you and I, Mississippi,
Rendezvoused two nights and days,
Browsing within the drowsing coverts

Of the unobtrusive cemetery
Consecrated to Grays who died in '62
From wounds at Shiloh and Brices Cross Roads

And where, later, at The Warehouse,
I transposed my silences into free verse,
Fades into hazy silhouettes.

Bailey's Woods, through which I traipsed,
Challenging my manhood,
Communing with Faulkner's lingering echoes,

Slips away over day's rim like the sun
Rappelling down night's velvet crevasse;
Rowan Oak looms yet, though vaguely,

In its Hellenic, antebellum elegance:
A green and white bouquet
Wilting by the minute in my eyes' grip.

These elusive mirages
I pursued with euphoric exuberance
All the way south out of time

And finally arrested long enough to penetrate
Have now come completely unshimmered.
The distance between them and me

Is an optical delusion so wide
Vision refuses to ponder their inaccessibility;
The dream recedes into disenchantment.

I shiver; my sallow, sweaty flesh
Belies a desiccated spirit.
Nothing is left except to bury myself

In solutidinous, useless work, writing poems,
Obligations casketing my fate,
And pray for occasional resurrections.

Chapter Seven

OXFORD'S DRY OASIS

On Safari

This beastly afternoon,
As I drive toward the equatorial mid-South,
My imagination is on safari
In search of migratory word-horde herds
That range between Perryville,
Sikeston, New Madrid, Blytheville, and Memphis
And drink at these oases periodically.

However, a hundred-fifty miles into the trip,
I've yet to catch so much as a glimpse
Of indigenous literary species —
Their poetic spots, stripes, rings, zigzags —
Or even suspect one in my vicinity.
Because of this season's drought,
They may have wandered much deeper south,

Seeking Delta tributaries, bayou food
Containing more Cajun spices —
Trial by fire as well as swamp water.
Whatever the cause, not a solitary word-herd stirs
As the miles unwind from the savannah
My mind evokes with growing urgency,
Thirsting to capture something to show for my work.

All day, I travel farther into the bush
Without spying tracks or droppings.
Finally, I arrive in Oxford, Mississippi,
Able to boast neither hide nor hair
Nor mythic horn from which ritual music soars
When a creature is gently trapped,
Then set loose for the sport of the quest.

Perhaps next time I decide to hunt on the run,
I'll pursue with increased diligence
Beasts within reach of my meager resources,
Such as "Man from Nantucket" limericks
And lavatory-door graffiti,
Not graceful, fleet-leaping free verse
Too distant and skittish for my low-power scope.

Auto-Biographia Literaria

Whether by the foot-wide floorboards
Seamed with rope, exposed roof beams
And square, hewn-timber ceiling supports,
Slat fans, antique chandeliers
Converted from kerosene to incandescent filaments,
Or stained-glass lunettes casting soft rose,
Amber, purple, green, cobalt-blue hues,
My shadow senses it's in familiar purlieus,
Welcomes blessed anonymity.

Perhaps the glass of Mouton-Cadet
My hand caresses sensuously,
Half-empty continually,
Is the sedative memory requires to allay anxieties
Arising whenever I range too distantly,
Briefly relocate my soul
In hope of finding my jettisoned past
Whispering to innocent faces in colored windows,
Mosaics in Oxford's temple walls.

Whatever the case, this place accepts me
Without questions, explanations,
Justifications for my peculiarly reclusive behavior,
Even though it appears I,
A middle-aged poet,
Carpetbagging troubadour,
Keep strange company with a Doppelgänger
Who rejects vested suit, dress shirt, and tie,
Instead dons jeans, workshirt, and boots.

Here in this God-forgotten desolation,
Where traces of the Great Scribe hover,
My spirit comes alive;
I write verse as though my life depends on it,
Knowing I'll die without any expectation of success,
Suspecting all the while
Creation is merely a pretense for surviving the night
By my self's self,
That soul within the Whole that craves posterity

Without the protocol and notoriety
Attending Nobel laureates
And repudiates celebrity in favor of abject neglect
For a chance at posthumous redemption.
Suddenly I realize why I've strayed so far
Just to cast my loneliest parts
To the darkling elements: it's my outsized ego
Desiring exercise, aspiring to stretch its singing wings
Over zones unflown since the Falconer died.

A Night in the Burying Place

To me, the strangest sensation
Is being totally alone in a familiar location,
Recognizing no faces all evening
Until, by inebriated stages,
The place assumes a vague, netherish reverberation
Whose echoing déjà vu connects the room
(This womb where, sipping Mouton-Cadet,
I record Vision's whispers)
To the Mother/Mistress/Muse,
That illusory effluvium which produces
Those who create from Silence's halo —
Through hands shaping clay,
Fingers with ink and paint forming strokes,
Notes, equations, tropes —
God-ladders, space-bridges, dream-domes.

Tonight, more poignantly than on most,
I sense this nexus
In the profoundly unrecognizable faces
Reveling about me in scattershot folly
And cloven-hoofed goat-lust.
I'm a gate-crasher at my own funeral,
Lone pallbearer shouldering my verse into apotheosis.
Although no better than other venues
For begetting brainchildren,
It's to Oxford, Mississippi,
The Warehouse, that I frequently gravitate
To release my earthly burdens
By burying them in my ledger
That they might disperse more easily into elements
Before soaring, reentering the Life Force.

Yet never has the raucous crowd
Seemed so somber
As it does this spectral evening,
Nor I so unaroused.
However, this land, necropolis, ossuary,
This night, this hour, this moment
*

Have served their purpose,
Are full, fallow, hollow, shallow, unhallowed
Embracing my stillborn imagination.
Tomorrow, I'll rise from bed dead
And resume my word-weary search
For a plot more conducive to natural childbirth.

Haunting Voices

I hear you. I hear you so near now
My ears grow numb to the noise
Disguised as animated conversation in this place
So far away from you;

Whether in a wind tunnel, diving bell,
Or just beyond Hell's perimeters,
From which emanates the most grotesque moaning,
I'd recognize your voices anywhere.

When it originates with his own guilt,
A parent rarely mistakes his children's cries
Or fails to identify their plaints
Laced with fear of being prematurely bereaved.

Tonight, my two little orphans,
I sense your silence; it pains me so
Knowing my separation from you
Must persist one day more

Before we'll all exist again
Within shouting distance of each other
Beneath the same roof,
Inside the Whitman Sampler house we occupy

Despite its effete, cliché-riddled mediocrity,
Which we rent by the month in St. Louis,
Where we've recently moved
To introduce you to better schooling.

Just one more reversal of my route
And I'll have obliterated Time,
Arrived again at that fated promontory
Where we embraced, kissed, cried, goodbyed

Without you realizing I'd die for three days,
Reenact a secular Passion Week
Before retreating to your sweet touching.
Tonight, I have no recourse

Except to endure in Oxford's Warehouse,
So distant from you,
Whose intuited voices my feverish ears
Isolate from white noise arcing across the room.

And I refuse to scratch through or revise my effort
To preserve you in my poetic loneliness,
Even if it is like freezing a mammoth in arctic ice,
Thawing it every few millennia.

Daydreaming of Night-Mares

What a quick shift my mind has made
Between the eyes' images this trip:
Cows, pigs, and feedcorn,
Transformed into sorghum, soybeans, cotton, and milo
With an artificer's invisible flourish,
Whose deft metaphoric trickery
Uplifts my spirit this out-of-sorts morning.

Going at my own pace, spaced out,
With no crusades importuning me,
Liberated from human ties, if not stress,
Arbitrariness deciding my nomadic destiny
And peripatetic vision,
I, Bellerophon, cruise low,
Hoping to avoid detection by Chimeras.

Having flown this southern route many times,
I'm certain fire-breathing creatures,
Part lion, serpent, goat,
Lurk behind kudzu, white shirt, and bow tie.
I swerve to make the Oxford exit.
Excited about reveling tonight
With Bacchus and Willie

And their cronies, Gambrinus and Falstaff,
I know before daybreak
I'll have drunk those heady reprobates
Under the table,
And, with dumb luck and the gods on my side,
I might even end up in bed
With a night-mare from The Warehouse's lusty stable.

"Counts No-Count"

For Willie Morris

Finding you again, so humble and accessible
Here in Oxford, coming slowly undone
In a sloe gin fizz, I grow wistful,
Wishing you and I might visit "Bill's" grave,
Press up against low-flying ghosts,
Resurrect his essence from night's dead center,
Mississippi's chrysalis,
And tell ourselves the heart has its eon
(Call it mini-death, if you will,
Or imaginative hiatus from Life)
In which to fulfill its primal destiny
Before committing itself to darkness.

Tonight, Willie,
You and I have connected
And, connecting, reminded each other
That some forms of self-expression
Require sketching, calligraphic swirling,
Yet others the tongue's deft strokes
To articulate compassion, evoke emotion,
The soul's passionate scratching on limestone.
Whatever monument-ality
We might salvage tomorrow morning
From this evening's subdued carousing
Remains for the future to assay.

All I can say for sure
Is that you, Willie, Yazoo City's chronicler,
And I, St. Louis' Jew poet,
Have blended our dispossessedness,
Reaffirmed the spirit's imperishability,
And in the process gotten completely blitzed,
The two of us
Just sodden, misbegotten practitioners of a craft
That has no relevance to the masses,
Who, by in large, regard us,
As they did "Billy" Faulkner of Oxford,
As "Count No-Count" bastards.

Failed Poet

What persistent images this misty town emits
For a visitor from distant northern regions,
Who sits drinking wine by the carafe
Upstairs, in a dark bar overlooking the Square,
Squinting through rain-splotched glass
At the illuminated, south-facing clock
Atop Lafayette County's courthouse,
Listening to "Rikki Don't Lose That Number,"
"Stairway to Heaven,"
The Moody Blues harmonizing "Nights in White Satin."

I submit to Oxford's incantatory, dizzy mysticism,
Dissolve like Alice and Lemuel
Through concentric hallucinations
Into a feculent, deliquescing whirlpool
No Odysseus dreamt of having to navigate
Nor the most tenacious, irate Ahab,
Misconstruing its swirl for a breaching white leviathan,
Harpoon poised on the tip of his bilious tongue,
Ever tried to row alongside
And single-handedly fling epithets at
For the sole sake
Of placating the soul's only self-justification:
Celebrating its immediate existence,
Saying "No!" to Death.

In this wet, warm pre-Christmas sky,
Visions of William Faulkner incandesce
Like fireflies exploding into obsolescence.
Peering out of the window, a Mad Hatter,
I'm inspired to turn into verse
My transported impressions,
Yet when I request fundamentals of the bartender —
Paper, pencil, peanuts,
One more glass of Napa Valley Chardonnay —
His quiet denial fractures concentration,
Stirs Ahab's hatred in my blood,
Returns me to Odysseus' dislocation
*

Here in this paltry oasis,
Where Faulkner gave free run to his demons,
Then disciplined them long enough
To make them dazed, crazed, ageless characters
For whom he'd allocate spaces
On the map of his New World, Yoknapatawpha,
Which he'd ultimately claim in the names of his queens,
Meta, Ruth, Joan, Jean, Else, and Estelle,
As did Christopher Columbus
For Ferdinand, Isabella, and their Savior.

I gaze out this rain-glazed second-story window,
Wondering how such a provincial "Billy"
Could have ever aspired to such creative heights,
Actually succeeded on the universal stage;
I'm amazed that his fiction was so widely praised
In a world inured to atom bombs,
German reparations, and a Cold War morality.
What I'm doing here this evening,
So far from my home and blessed children, I can't say.

Perhaps, like an archaeologist,
I've arrived in town to establish new digs,
Discover ancient ruins
Which might reveal newer ruins,
Afford clues and speculations
As to how human civilizations evolve
And individual imaginations proliferate
Despite all odds,
Transliterate from modern Rosetta stones
"A Rose for Emily," *The Sound and the Fury*, "The Bear,"
And thereby gain insight into an entire culture
Previously undisclosed.

Here in Oxford, Mississippi, tonight, right now,
I try to locate my ghost in proximity to Faulkner's
And, balking like a fractious donkey,
Accept second-class status,
Resign myself to inferior lights,
*

Get so drunk I trip down the stairs on leaving,
Weave back to the Alumni House,
And drop into bed
With my clothes still clinging to my sweaty body,
Knowing I'm doomed the rest of my life
To write my guts into poetry
No one will buy, read, recite, teach,
Let alone remember.

The Hazards of Road Traveling

To Jackson and back this bleak, gray-black day,
I've traveled in the backwash and suck
Of freighted tractor-trailers
Slicing the highway with their implacable velocity,
Spraying my windshield with such blinding tidal thrusts
My eyes flinch,
My hands strangle the wheel,
My entire body shudders;
And even though this distracting splatter
Fails to inundate my station wagon,
I feel its wetness saturate me,
As if I'm bleeding from the outside in
Through sweating flesh and porous bones
Barely keeping my lacerated imagination dry.

Now, although returned physically to Oxford,
Uncertainties persist;
Those grisly premonitions of death
And peripatetic uprootedness,
Which motion engenders in the perpetual waif
Who carries on his shoulder from Hell to Hell
Hurdy-gurdy and the snail's shell,
Circle back like a hound-scurried rabbit,
Crash head-on, at a dead run, into my stranded spirit.
Predictably, I react to my own time-lapsed mortality;
Wine-drenched and dizzy
In the lighted aura of the Courthouse,
I realize exactly when Death's screeching vulture
Grabbed me and soared.

It all started so innocently, so unanticipated,
That first time I set out from Farmington on my own,
Kissed goodbye my wife,
Sweetly drowsing in innocent dreams,
Touched the twitching eyelids of my baby girl
Sleeping in the same bed
To protect her from winged monkeys,
And headed off for Oxford like Don Quixote,
*

With chivalric vexations, to save distressed maidens,
Tilt against windmills,
And locate and stake in my alien name
Whatever unknown Cíbola or Carcassonne
Might remain to be charted in northern Mississippi.
Paradoxically, that's when the end began.

These lonesome, spendthrift days,
Memory itself is mere flotsam.
My wasted energy accumulates like bat dung in caves,
Gull guano on atolls.
No one knows under which alias I come and go,
Neither ladies in waiting nor the one who bore my issue
Before our hearts' brass ring tarnished,
Their painted ponies flaked.
Tonight, gazing at the gaily Christmas-lit Square,
Focusing closer, farther from home than ever,
On honey-glazed, Ole Miss coed cunts
Flaunting their silken-haired wares in eternal heat,
I see how really dreadful the prospect is
Of growing old already dead.

Chapter Eight

HEADING NORTHWARD HOME

Seeking a Change of Venue

Halfway through April,
This region's trees have awakened,
Begun greening: peacocks haughtily preening,
Flaunting dogwood dazzlements,
Stipple-dappling the eye pink and white.

Only somnolent kudzu,
Barely perceptible for its charcoal drapes
Clinging thinly to the landscape
Like attenuated strands of Spanish moss,
Has failed to assume tumescence.

As I head toward Memphis from Oxford,
Metaphor transports my morose spirit
Through a series of hallucinatory orbits,
Each circling the same core:
Northern Mississippi.

I am, in various earthly guises,
Henry Sutpen, Quentin Compson, Jackson Fentry,
And ten-year-old Ike McCaslin.
I am, at 42, an adolescent
Lacking wisdom to set myself free,

Needing prescience, humor, fortitude
To find my way into,
Not out of, the darkling Woods
And there locate truth's numinous luminosity
Looming like giant stallions and bears in the gloom.

For too many seasons,
My psyche has refused to do blood rites,
Neglected tribal sacrifices,
Conspired with Society to hide in its soft folds
Like chlamydia, undetected by its host.

I've paraded naked, fully clothed, in broad daylight,
Gone by two names simultaneously,
Benbow/Bond,
An intensely intellectual moron
Groping for a solution to my own ambiguities,

A nexus from the Edge into the depths,
Where growing up and focusing in
Converge on intuition,
And loving someone other than Self
Becomes the heart's singular passion and pursuit.

I've pondered these bleak, dire requirements
Entirely too long
Without being able to conclude them
Or reconcile their irresoluteness.
Perhaps this is why I've driven to Mississippi

With such frequency: to beseech its phantoms
To treat me without the harsh partiality
I display in judging myself
And pray, by pleading poetic insanity,
They'll forgive, if not acquit, my meager ego.

Getting Butterflies

Already, the thick Mississippi air
Is astir with April's first flush
Of butterflies.
They drift and hover
Like dreams riding slipstreams
Toward certain finalities.
We converge. The silent crash
Of insects impacting grill and bumper
Sets up a painful pounding
So loud inside my head
I might be taking ak-ak flak
To the vital psyche.
Sinister premonitions explode,
Vaporize around me like cyanide pellets,
Honeycombed anxieties,
Then dissolve.
Queasy, I tremble with guilt
For inescapably maiming and annihilating
Nature's gentlest creatures.
All the way home,
As though suffering a nervous tic,
My eyes flick from the road
To rearview mirror;
My head continuously twists
Back over my shoulder,
Possibly to catch a split-second re-
Flection of a juggernaut
Fate might be shoving toward me
From behind,
On whose grill and bumper
I'll be splattered.

Flying Too Low to Avoid Detection

Having driven out of Oxford in an amnesic lapse
All the way past Memphis to Osceola,
I awaken like fabled Ursa Major,
Peer earthward at day's night-sky,
Survey the moon-pocked space I occupy.
Hovering on rigid wax wings,
My downcast shadow shudders
As if waiting to muster the courage to leap,
Fly free, clear an invisible abyss
Dividing my present destiny
From previous Red Sea oppressions.

But unlike inspired Icarus,
I can't even construct a winged metaphor
To let me soar high enough
To at least bruise myself falling,
Arrive home with proof I've encountered the enemy,
Some tangible excuse
By which I might acquit myself,
In my wife's unforgiving eyes,
Of deliberately engaging in disreputable pursuits
Or honestly deny
I'm purposely trying to undo our sacred ties.

The Profligate Jew Returns

Although no inordinately compelling designs
Motivate or guide me,
My collapsed psyche, like Icarus' wax wings
Failing to hacksaw the sun's rays,
Plummets into a northern Red Sea.
I'm afraid that not even negative motion
Can save me from gravity's shear,
Keep reality's tidal wave from drowning me
Before I'm washed ashore
And seen no more amidst its shifting sands.

Having traveled seven hours by dead reckoning,
I finally approach St. Louis;
Arrival frightens me awake
With disorienting horror.
Something about Missouri's thin April air
Causes tight breathing, chest pains.
Instinctively, I take Highway 40's Hanley exit,
Head north, then east half a mile,
Until I reach my driveway
And the car dies into silence.

Suddenly I intuit why, for three days,
I've not realized this unholy pilgrimage
Has been just another sacrilegious reenactment
Of my heart's Passion Week.
Home again to my empty temple, I weep.

Biographical Note

Louis Daniel Brodsky was born in St. Louis, Missouri, in 1941, where he attended St. Louis Country Day School. After earning a B.A., magna cum laude, at Yale University in 1963, he received an M.A. in English from Washington University in 1967 and an M.A. in Creative Writing from San Francisco State University the following year.

Mr. Brodsky is the author of twenty-one volumes of poetry, four of which have been published in French by Éditions Gallimard. His poems have appeared in many publications, including *Harper's*, *Southern Review*, *Texas Quarterly*, *National Forum*, *Ariel*, *American Scholar*, *Kansas Quarterly*, Ball State University's *Forum*, *New Welsh Review*, *Cimarron Review*, *Orbis*, and *Literary Review*, as well as in five editions of the *Anthology of Magazine Verse and Yearbook of American Poetry*.

Also available from **Time Being Books**®

LOUIS DANIEL BRODSKY
You Can't Go Back, Exactly
The Thorough Earth
Four and Twenty Blackbirds Soaring
Mississippi Vistas: Volume One of *A Mississippi Trilogy*
Falling from Heaven: Holocaust Poems of a Jew and a Gentile
  (with William Heyen)
Forever, for Now: Poems for a Later Love
Mistress Mississippi: Volume Three of *A Mississippi Trilogy*
A Gleam in the Eye: Poems for a First Baby
Gestapo Crows: Holocaust Poems
The Capital Café: Poems of Redneck, U.S.A.

HARRY JAMES CARGAS (Editor)
Telling the Tale: A Tribute to Elie Wiesel on the Occasion of
  His 65th Birthday — Essays, Reflections, and Poems

ROBERT HAMBLIN
From the Ground Up: Poems of One Southerner's Passage to
  Adulthood

WILLIAM HEYEN
Falling from Heaven: Holocaust Poems of a Jew and a Gentile
  (with Louis Daniel Brodsky)
Erika: Poems of the Holocaust
Pterodactyl Rose: Poems of Ecology
Ribbons: The Gulf War — A Poem
The Host: Selected Poems 1965-1990

TED HIRSCHFIELD
German Requiem: Poems of the War and the Atonement of a
Third Reich Child

VIRGINIA V. JAMES HLAVSA
Waking October Leaves: Reanimations by a Small-Town Girl

RODGER KAMENETZ
The Missing Jew: New and Selected Poems

NORBERT KRAPF
Somewhere in Southern Indiana: Poems of Midwestern Origins

ADRIAN C. LOUIS
Blood Thirsty Savages

JOSEPH MEREDITH
Hunter's Moon: Poems from Boyhood to Manhood

TIME BEING BOOKS®
POETRY IN SIGHT AND SOUND

FOR OUR FREE CATALOG OR TO ORDER

(800) 331-6605 Monday through Friday
8 a.m. to 4 p.m. Central time
FAX: (314) 432-7939